God's Blanket of Love

Spiritual poems reflecting testimonies from people who shared their life changing experiences

Written by

Deirdre Mebane

Copyright © 2013 Deirdre Mebane

All rights reserved.

ISBN-10: 149362847X
ISBN-13: 978-1493628476

DEDICATION

I dedicate this book in memory of family members who are no longer with us but had a tremendous religious affect on my life: father, Rev. Dr. J.R. Hampton, mother-in-law Malinda T. Mebane, grandparents Rev. and Mrs. J.B. Hampton and Mr. and Mrs. J.E. Williamson

CONTENTS

	Acknowledgments	Pg 6
1	God's Blanket of Love	Pg 8
2	A Tragedy That Directs Her Path	Pg 9
3	An One Time God	Pg 10
4	Blessed With A Special Mom	Pg 11
5	Bringing God's Word Alive	Pg 12
6	Come Get Fed At The Table	Pg 13
7	God Answers Prayers	Pg 14
8	God Blessed Them With Three	Pg 15
9	God Heals A Youth	Pg 16-17
10	He's A Miracle Worker	Pg 17
11	Let Go And Let God	Pg 18

CONTENTS

12	Rejoicing Through A Trial	Pg 19
13	Be Encouraged	Pg 20
14	God Awakes A Deep Sleep	Pg 21
15	God's Benefits Are Sweet	Pg 22
16	Saved By God's Shield	Pg 23
17	God's Holla To Youth	Pg 24-25
18	Praise God For Each Other	Pg 25-26
19	Prayers Go Up Blessings Come Down	Pg 26-27
20	There Is Peace For The Weary	Pg 27-28
21	Unleash Your Hidden Talents	Pg 28
22	What Choice Will You Make	Pg 29
23	Mom Is Always There	Pg 30
23	Packed For The Journey	Pg 30-31
24	God's Holla Back To The Youth	Pg 31-32
25	A Magnificent View	Pg 33
26	Believe You Will Receive	Pg 34
27	Just Be Thankful To God	Pg 35
28	Is Your Passport Ready	Pg 36
29	Men Molded By God	Pg 37
30	About The Author	Pg 38

ACKNOWLEDGMENTS

First I give honor to God for making this book possible. I thank Him for revealing a hidden talent that only He knew existed. Growing closer to God I hear the words He wants me to put into poetic form and to share with others. I thank Him for all the people He brought me in contact with to bring these poems to life.

I thank my husband Tyrone for being patient and a good listener while this book was being created. I would like to also thank my Mother, Mary, sisters Sheinita and Denise, brother-in-law Jimmie, aunt Diane, uncle JP, Dad Mebane, sister-in-law Michelle, brother-in-law Vince, nieces Briana, Crystal, Kaela and nephew James. Your continued support means the world to me and I love you all very dearly. Thank you Rev. Dr. Howard L. Woods, Jr, pastor, for encouraging me to continue writing and using my poems at church.

GOD'S BLANKET OF LOVE
(Written: 2005)

When troubles seem to weigh you down

God's strength will always be around

When sickness seems to fill your soul

God's healing hands will take control

When grief of a loved one is too much to bear

God's blanket of love will comfort with care

When the sins of the world try to change your faith

Read God's Holy word, it will set things straight

When all else fails and fear is subdued

Put on God's Holy Armor

For He always sees you through

A TRAGEDY THAT DIRECTS HER PATH
(Written: 2005)

The Tarpley's moved from the west to the east in 1975

Wife and husband of 14 years plus two kids by their side

In disbelief their world was shattered in 1977

Tragedy struck this family taking one soul to heaven

Her husband, the experienced hunter left the house one day

Got in his truck, drove down the road, rejoicing all the way

Knew not the day nor the hour until he heard a call

Accidentally his gun went off and suddenly there was a fall

God appeared held out his hand motioning time to go

Left behind his wife and kids saying it isn't so

Shock and rage filled her soul over the lost of her man

Why did God reach out and quickly take his hand

God whispered Sister Tarpley just be strong

With power and grace He gave her a new song

Go live with your children to receive their care

God will see that she safely makes it there

Leaving the Ebenezer family and the pastor to

God will direct her path and see her through

A sweet, kind and gentle woman thankful each day

I dedicate this poem to her in my own special way

AN ONE TIME GOD
(Written 2005)

Discovery of a lump turned into a scare

Doctors unconcerned watched her with care

A year went by then another cyst appeared

Nervous of the results as her surgery drew near

The doctor advised he had the answer

The lump they removed did have cancer

During church service to the altar she went

Receiving special prayers was time well spent

Medication and radiation is the next step to do

Believing that God would see her through

The doctors feel confident she will be fine

She knew for sure that God is always on time

Her Brother did say with a smile on his face

God healed her body with His saving grace

BLESSED WITH A SPECIAL MOM
(Written: 2005)

Our Mom is very special to us

Providing for her family without a fuss

Knows what we need before we do

Mom's intuition protects us too

Became Mother and Father after Dad died

All of us empty and lonely inside

God surrounded us with love and care

Intense family bond now we share

Mom's musical talent masters any song

We join in harmony while singing along

Grandchildren bring joy, laughter and smiles

Mom loves to spoil them regardless of the miles

Blessed with a Mom who's beautiful and smart

We really love you from the bottom of our hearts

BRINGING GOD'S WORD ALIVE
(Written: 2005)

He's building the Ark one soul at a time

Teaching the gospel absorbing each mind

Vividly bringing God's word alive

Sensing His Spirit deep down inside

No script or notes just a Bible in hand

Plainly delivers so even a child would understand

Souls have traveled just to hear him speak

New ones joining almost every week

A heritage of pastors many stories to tell

Following strong footsteps and doing so well

Ebenezer loves and adores him trusting in God's plan

Grateful we're blessed with this dedicated man

COME GET FED AT THE TABLE
(Written: 2005)

Growing up Sunday dinners were a tradition

Home cook meals enjoyed in dining rooms and kitchens

Head of the table ready to say grace

Families gather quickly to take their place

Helpings of love, devotion, obedience and prayer

Reminiscence of God's blessings soon fills the air

Fully satisfied collapsing into a light sleep

Who started these traditions the ones we keep

It was the Messiah always willing and able

Calling several thousand to get fed at the table

His most important meal happened ages in the past

Advising his disciples that would be the last

Peter asked why Jesus was on bended knee

John 13:8 says, "If you wash thee not, thou has no part of me"

Learn at the table traditions are food for the soul

Keep God first, Keep traditions active, Keeps us spiritually whole

GOD ANSWERS PRAYERS
(Written: 2005)

Life causes confusion

Hinders support and trust

If you want prayers to be answered

Loving God is a must

Close your eyes and just listen

He is speaking to you

He hears all of your cries

He understands them too

He will protect and guide your needs

Open your heart and let Him in

God does answer prayers

In Him you can depend

GOD BLESSED THEM WITH THREE
(Written: 2005)

A special couple united in marriage

Naturally wanted to fill a baby carriage

Their love for one another is very strong

They had no idea anything was wrong

The news came they could not conceive

Three separate times they became bereaved

Disappointed and hurt as any parent would be

They cried to God and He heard their plea

They prayed and prayed for a positive change

Knowing their faith would help them sustain

Many medical trials were used for this goal

God kept them close deep down to their souls

The exciting news had them so full of tears

Now with three little ones after so many years

Filled with joy they gave God all the praise

Three bundles of joy they will now get to raise

God was not finished with this plan you see

He blessed them with little ones a total of three

GOD HEALS A YOUTH
(Written: 2005)

Josh loves sports he loves to play

Had no idea things wouldn't go his way

Tired and weak his chest tightened fast

Heart beating quickly how long will this last

Doctors ran test to see what they could do

Unhappy with the results and needing surgery too

Josh was upset his family felt the same

Was he ever going to be able to play the game

Went to church and Elder Kelly took a stand

Praying over Josh while grasping his hand

Holy oil and prayer anointed his face

Faith was the preparation for this race

Went through surgery totally aware

This operation was suppose to be a repair

5 hours later the doctors were stunned

No problems showing once surgery begun

Excited with the news that he was okay

Realizing God healed him all the way

Youth think testimonies come from the old

Never understanding until they've been told

Reality hits when it comes from a peer

Josh told his story for youthful ears to hear

HE'S A MIRACLE WORKER
(Written: 2005)

You hurt, you cry, your pain is strong

You call on Jesus to ask what is wrong

Pain like lightening striking fast

Moans sounding like thunder imagine that

Tingling feelings down your arm

Now is the time to get alarmed

Sharp piercing pain across your back

Not really sure if it is an attack

Rushed to the doctor for his advice

Quick ride to the hospital not thinking twice

You called on Jesus to fix what is wrong

A sense of calmness now makes you strong

Baffled by the test the doctors said can't be

Jesus stepped in and healed her quickly

Always call on Jesus no matter how you feel

He's a miracle worker always seeking to heal

LET GO AND LET GOD
(Written: 2005)

A long time ago there was a young boy

He had a good childhood filled with much joy

Called as a follower and this is what he heard

Go spread the gospel and preach my Holy word

He entered the ministry very eager to learn

To teach others about God was his main concern

Some souls were saved and some turned away

God kept him focused and positive each day

He sang "Christ is all He's everything to me"

As humble as he knew how and trusting in Thee

Let go and let God the most remembered speech

Let God take total control is what he preached

Blessed with a wife and three girls all were proud

Angelic and powerful voice would draw any crowd

He went home to God for his task was completed

He fulfilled his dream and did what was needed

Great memories to share to create a warm grin

He was a great pastor, husband, father and friend

REJOICING THROUGH A TRIAL
(Written: 2005)

That morning James drifted unconsciously to sleep

He showed no response and we began to weep

Confined to a hospital connected to machines

Never sick like this before what did this mean

Family came together for support and prayer

Knowing that God will always be there

Side effects made his infant body weak

His stay started as days then became weeks

Both hospitals' staff worked hard and fast

Best medical care received now is in his past

God was there from the halls to James' room

Presence of His Spirit offering healing soon

God shapes our character like a Potter would

Sending us through phases well understood

Rejoice in your trials God will handle the rest

Rejoicing helps others going through personal distress

BE ENCOURAGED
(Written: 2006)

Be encouraged seek God's love

He rewards us from above

Be encouraged without doubt

Reading His Word will help us out

Be encouraged ask for His command

Hold tight don't let go of His unchanging hand

Be encouraged when things go wrong

Listen to testimonies they make us strong

Be encouraged visit God's temple

It brings understanding more clear and simple

Be encouraged the battle is not yours

All hardships belong to the Lord's

Be encouraged open up your heart

Admit loving Jesus now is your start

Be encouraged be born again

Through baptism he'll remove your sins

Be encouraged life is just a test

Be encouraged He always knows what's best

GOD AWAKES A DEEP SLEEP
(Written: 2006)

Imagine your life controlled by ventilation

Two stories from two women worth celebration

Saints came together praising God's name

Would these two ladies ever be the same

No movement no talking as time went by

God came to visit and His reason why

Responded in time knowing just what to do

No help does He need to see His plan through

God whispered to them saying don't weep

Because of your faith I'll awake your sleep

Saints from everywhere prayed in numbers

God woke them up from their deep slumbers

These ladies came to church what a time we shared

Their miracles of life returned with such care

GOD'S BENEFITS ARE SWEET
(Written: 2006)

Bad things in life temp us to stray

Grasping to pull us the wrong way

Who do you turn to during despair

Burdens so heavy no one can bear

So many issues overwhelm us inside

Call on Jesus or give up which to decide

Stop and think where our lives would be

Without God's blessings He gives tenderly

No healing, no miracles, no love to give

A world of sadness is no place to live

There's hope and happiness good news to us

God protects and gives as long as we trust

Love Him and call Him every day we can

God stretches out his unchanging hands

Now despair bounces off like a breeze

Walls of armor embrace us with ease

God knows our needs before we think

He erases those burdens in a blink

God graciously gives to everyone we meet

God's love is genuine and His benefits are sweet

SAVED BY GOD'S SHIELD
(Written: 2006)

Pray every morning for a protective fence

For my entire family and friends for them to sense

The sounds of gospel start my day

Quiet mediation to God I pray

Driving to work in darkness no fear

Confident that God is always near

Passenger window quickly shatters

Called the police to research this matter

Now it is clear someone shot at the car

From a dark distance not very far

God spoke and said "no need for alarm"

"Look and see that you're not harmed"

Saved by God's shield completely that day

Forming rays of protection against harm's way

GOD'S HOLLA TO THE YOUTH
(Written: 2007)

Wuz up my peeps do you really know me

I'm not a gangster found on BET

What's popping these days I don't hear your call

Hanging out with your friends at different malls

You say that pressures are weighing you down

I can bring you out but you must come around

Let me ask you some questions to help you believe

All the good things from God you've received

Ever been in trouble and safely got out

It was God, the One without a doubt

Ever received a gift that may have been hiding

It was God's blessings, His way of providing

Ever broken bones, had a cold or the flu

It was God's healing that brought you through

Ever offered something you knew not to take

You think serving time is a big mistake

Ever been pressured to be in the crowd

Ever heard a voice saying NO pretty loud

Ever been driving or riding and just missed danger

That's God intervening the Devil's anger

It's normal to feel sad but you can be happy too

Just talk to God, He will answer you

Just chill your parents know what is right

Even though you think it's always a fight

God will always protect your back

Just trust in His word it's a matter of fact

Hey......Holla back soon

Special thanks to Briana H, Sherdena J and Fallon R for your help!

PRAISE GOD FOR EACH OTHER
(Written: 2007)

Do you remember your very first date

Not of your past ones but of your mate

Ponder over memories revealing very clear

A blooming relationship that started over years

Days change to years as the time goes by

Tension in the household can't explain why

Blaming each other resulting in a holler

Over simple things a bill or even a dollar

Pressures of the world break down your soul

Allowing the devil's schemes to take control

But God steps in and says don't lash out that's not the key

Only God's Armor strengthens like a wall

No one can remove it unless you fall

Couples stay together for years with a reason

Trusting God first everyday every season

Rekindle Christian love don't wait start now

Share quiet togetherness anyway any how

Hold your spouse's hand and gaze in their eyes

Praise God for each other and all God provides

follow me

PRAYERS GO UP BLESSINGS COME DOWN
(Written: 2007)

We are so blessed with a loving Father

Call Him constantly no sense of bother

God wants us to depend on Him

During great times and when things look grim

The best way to communicate is simple as can be

Prayer yes prayer definitely is the key

We pray for everyone in any situations found

When prayers go up to God blessings do come down

We take prayers seriously because we truly know

Prayers make things better and help our faith grow

There's so many examples of bad turned into good

Rejoicing in the miracles rejoicing as we should

Just like in the Bible days Jesus did perform

Sight, life and deliverance healing to conform

Miracles are still occurring each and everyday

God is proof He is the light, truth and the way

Still don't believe in miracles then look around and see

All the people who struggled who now have been set free

THERE IS PEACE FOR THE WEARY
(Written: 2007)

There is peace for the weary you can have it today

There is peace for the weary if your soul's gone astray

You can smile now forever only one thing to do

Give your burdens to Jesus let Him carry you

Worry is the worst sin it's dangerous and seeks

People down and out who are spiritually weak

Worry wants to own you mind, body and soul

Jesus has the power to demolish that control

There is peace for the weary you can have it today

There is peace for the weary if your soul's gone astray

You can smile now forever only one

Give your burdens to Jesus let Him carry you

Once worry is gone you're given a second chance

Confident and peaceful makes you want to dance

Glorifying Jesus helps to carry you

Removing tough situations that you went through

There is peace for the weary you can have it today

There is peace for the weary if your soul's gone astray

You can smile now forever only one thing to do

Give all your burdens to Jesus let Him carry you

UNLEASED YOUR HIDDEN TALENTS
(Written: 2007)

We were reminded to focus on our goals

Listen, observe, activate supportively we're told

The greatest part is simple and absolutely true

The talents God observed are the things you love to do

God is asking us, what you do your best

List those favorite tasks separate from the rest

These are your hidden talents right before your eyes

Talents God has given you no secret or surprise

These talents were hidden waiting to come out

You have to trust in God, completely without doubt

When you release your talents then you'll realize

Emphasize your favorite ones not the ones despised

Share with others what God has shared with you

Support is critical to see this mission through

WHAT CHOICE WILL YOU MAKE
(Written: 2007)

Do you know who God is

Have you brought Him in your heart

Do you know His word is true

Reading the scriptures is a start

Do you know that you can trust Him

No matter how hard the test

Do you know how much He loves you

When you feel life is but a mess

Do you know God is your Father

To protect through thick and thin

Do you know God can erase

Fallen short and full of sin

Do you know you'll have a choice

In the future for your sake

Who will you follow what choice will you make

Do you know it's not too late

Joining God's family is the right thing to do

Now you know that God really cares

He loves and believes in you

MOM IS ALWAYS THERE
(Written: 2008)

A God fearing woman who lives by the book

Will set your actions straight with that staring look

Like her Mother and Grandmother she prays for all

Praying for protection and no harm to fall

Took the family to church so they can learn

How Jesus directs her path and provides what's earned

A struggle to Mom when we questioned what's right

Acting too grown for ourselves wanting to move out of sight

Discovered in time Mom's knowledge was true

Not something simple she made up out of the blue

Mom is always there to mend all wounds

Acting as Mother and Father making you feel better soon

She has a strong bond that can handle any test

God blessed us with Moms who knows what's best

PACKED FOR THE JOURNEY
(Written: 2008)

Traveling down the road of life

Can be difficult if you don't pack

Not just a toothbrush or your favorite clothes

But spiritual things to keep you on track

Neatly fold wisdom, charity, forgiveness and love

These important things will fit better than a glove

No need for a GPS to help you find your way

Place your Bible on top for its contents saves the day

What's missing any other things from the upper room

Hurry up, get ready, God will arrive soon

Don't forget to carry faith to share with those in need

Helping others find their way, empty souls to feed

Now you're packed for the journey, but you will be missed

Similar goals we share God's kingdom we seek

You're ready to go with the talents God gave you

Talents so special and truly unique

GOD'S HOLLA BACK TO THE YOUTH
(Written: 2012)

What's up my young people

I came back to see

Why you are judging others

When that task belongs to me

You're steadily getting angry

Over one's popularity

Ready to roll up on them

With no common sense or clarity

Remember I made you in my image

For that you should be glad

You should love and just be chillin'

Instead of getting mad

I am the one you will face

To discuss your earthly faults

I decide your fate

If over Jordan you will cross

So while I'm here to visit

You remember this for thought

Being jealous against all others

Is not the love I taught

Come to me when you're troubled

Stop hating on your friends

I have the final say so

Where your soul rest in the end

Holla back always. God

A special thanks to my nieces Briana and Crystal for their help!

A MAGNIFICENT VIEW
(Written: 2012)

Oh I wish you could see this magnificent view

As I stand by the Creator looking down upon you

He knew it was time to take me by hand

Streets paved with gold as my entrance was planned

As I sit by the river Jordan looking out to see

All of God's angels welcoming me

I'm already settled into this grand place

I will never forget each and every face

The music they play is my favorite songs

I cannot wait to sing long

I love you so much and we shared so many things

Oh I wish you could see my beautiful wings

I'm in my new place so many new things to do

Oh I wish you could see this magnificent view

BELIEVE YOU WILL RECEIVE
(Written: 2012)

God says ask and it shall be given

But do we seek so we can find

Do we not listen to God's talking

As issues fall further behind

Have you faced major obstacles

You tried to handled on your own

Have you ask God to fix them

Or further become withdrawn

When you pray and ask for help

You have to trust it will come through

Hold God to His written word

While in praying you can do

Once you've prayed your request

Let God take care of the rest

No matter how big or small

Remember God can handle it all

Believe and you will receive

Seek so you can find

Meditate the doors will open then

God will say the issue is mine

JUST BE THANKFUL TO GOD
(Written: 2012)

Clothes on your back and a roof overhead

Arise on your own to a full table spread

God sent His son to forgive all our sins

Erasing them all from beginning to end

Just be thankful to God

Elders are present to teach all they know

Sharing very special stories helping us grow

Parents put in place to show us right from wrong

Protecting with all their strength and supporting all along

Just be thankful to God

Praying to hear God speaking to you

Avoiding life's disasters with protection too

Honest Christian role models help to build your faith

Be willing and open to listen for ignoring is a big mistake

Just be thankful to God

How do you turn discouragement to happiness and joy

Focus your eyes on Jesus his grace and mercy can restore

Move from how people make you feel to what you really know

God's a keeper and supplier so act right and let it show

Just be thankful to God

IS YOUR PASSPORT READY
(Written: 2012)

Have you done all the things you are supposed to do

Are you lending a helping hands and saying positive things too

Have you wondered what is would be like

To see the look upon His face

To fall at His feet giving thanks for His saving grace

A long golden train descends from above

Surrounded by angels and beautiful white doves

Trumpets fill the air then a carpet rolls out

Take a seat upfront and learn what this journey is all about

Riding with several others the winds keep this train steady

An angel touches your hand asking if your passport is ready

Crossover the river Jordan my eyes do behold

The most luxurious pearls on a gate of pure gold

Hear your name called asking if you passed the test

God nods His head enter in no time to rest

What a time you will have as relatives guide you around by hand

To see your new surroundings get acquainted with God's land

Remember to do what's right your itinerary will be your guide

All you need is yourself and your service

Everything else God will provide

MEN MOLDED BY GOD
(Written: 2012)

God took moist clay and turned it into man

Sent them to be leaders was God's command

Leaders of families' protection of the home

Making sure the contents inside suspiciously don't roam

Strong, devoted God fearing is man

Born of God's image to be leaders of the land

Men should set examples of right and wrong

Turning boys to men faithful and strong

Men are molded by God the first human race

Are you committed to run God's race

God created woman to be unique to each man

She must love God and truly understand

Men are molded by God to rule the land and sea

To fear God, to keep things straight and to be the best they can be

ABOUT THE AUTHOR

I was born in a Christian loving family in Sanford, NC. My family consisted of my parents, my two sisters and myself. My father and his father were both ministers. I learn and accepted Jesus as my personal Savior at a very early age. It was not until I became older that I began to understand what it meant to be delivered through tough situations until I heard people speak about their trials and tribulations and how Jesus brought them through it. I learned firsthand through my own trials and it deepen my faith that as long as we trust God with all our hearts and minds that His will would be done.

God has shown me how He can give you gifts and talents you never knew existed within your soul. God can take you completely out of your comfort zone to reveal the most incredible gifts created only for you personally to bless others. We have to trust God and pray constantly to ask for guidance to do His will to the best if our abilities.

This book was created after listening to many testimonies from Christians and to bless others that may have gone through the same situation or are going through. God says, "Trust in the Lord with all thine heart; and lean not unto thine own understanding. In all thy ways acknowledge Him, and He shall direct thy paths." Proverbs 3:5-6

Made in the USA
Coppell, TX
11 January 2022